Trash Talking to God

A 40 DAY DEVOTIONAL GUIDE

Kevin Tully

Introduction

I am a runner. I'm not as fast as I used to be, and I can't run as far as I once could, but I am still a runner. For the past thirty years, I've mixed cycling, swimming, and weightlifting into my exercise regimen, but I still run an average of three days a week. It's convenient, less expensive than other sports I enjoy, elegantly simple, and childishly fun.

On the days I run, I walk the first few blocks to stretch my legs a little; after my run, I begin my cool-down about half a mile away from my starting and ending place—usually home. The miles running benefit my body. The last half-mile benefits my soul. In fact, the last half-mile is often the most deeply spiritual part of my day. That's when I pick up the trash.

I don't pick up all the trash I see along the way while cooling down. After all, I have a schedule to keep, and I must get to the other things I have planned for the day. Sometimes I feel disgusted by what I see thrown onto the street or into the ditch. There are times I pick up trash until my hands are full...so until I get to a trash can or Dumpster, I have to walk past some trash I can't carry at that moment. But those instances of walking past trash are deeply spiritual moments too. It's been a profoundly enlightening experience to discover that trash is a good symbol for so many other things in life. For example, in the case of the trash I have to leave when my hands are full: every day there are matters I would like to tackle but I cannot because of prior commitment, lack of resources, or time constraints. Most people I know can relate to that predicament. So picking up trash is kind of like...*life.*

I often wonder about how the trash got there and about the person who put it there. Has that person never been taught? Did he or she simply do what was convenient? Was it a case of being told, "Just throw it out," by someone he or she was riding with? Is it the result of a careless toss toward a trash can that didn't hit the target but wasn't corrected? My talks with God about the trash tend to raise a lot of questions that correlate to situations in other areas of life: Why is there crime? Why do we humans so often do what's convenient instead of what's right? Am I as conscious as I should be about how simple inattention can lead to problems in our own and others' lives? Do words that I carelessly speak create blight and harm for others? When my words miss the goal of helping, do I leave them lying there or do I quickly make the effort to correct my mistake?

This Lenten season, I invite you into a series of meditations about a few of my discoveries, conversations, and reflections while trash-talking with God. Most of these conversations I have had on multiple occasions, as I ponder repetitive situations concerning me, my life, God, trash, and the world. Some of the conversations are like earlier ones but are somehow evolving. In these cases, it's as if the trash keeps on happening but I have become different. At other times, the opposite is true: the trash is new, but my feelings and attitudes about the situations are the same ones I've wrestled with before...and ones in which I sense God wrestling with me. Sort of like a lot else in my life.

The image of "trash" is literal in the writings. But for you, it may be symbolic of something else in your life. Whether it's been thrown your way by someone else or something that seems to present itself anew in various forms every day, I hope you'll be able to sense the universal connection we all have with the trash we encounter as we seek to live as citizen-stewards of the planet and as the people of God.

Ash Wednesday

Read Galatians 5:13–15

For you have been called to live in freedom, my brothers and sisters. But don't use your freedom to satisfy your sinful nature. Instead, use your freedom to serve one another in love. For the whole law can be summed up in this one command: "Love your neighbor as yourself."

(Galatians 5:13–14 NLT)

I've been picking up trash at the end of my run for more than ten years now. As I talk to God about the trash I see and about the people who put it there, my conversations have led me to three inescapable reasons I ought to pick up the trash, and—for me, at least—must keep doing so:

1. I'm there.
2. I can.
3. It seems like the right thing to do.

Thus, the moment when I see the trash is something of a test. It's not a trial, not a burden, but simply a test. It shows who I am in that moment. Am I the kind of person who sees a problem and walks past, hoping someone else will take care of it? Or am I someone who will do something to help, even though it seems a mere drop in the proverbial bucket? The moment I am there with the trash is an adventure, really. Here I am, at this moment that has never existed, with this situation before me. It's there, and I'm here. I can do something to help, or I can choose not to. (There are usually good arguments on both sides of that one.) But the third of the aforementioned reasons always leads me to respond to the extent that I can. If I walk past without doing anything about the trash, I am (in that moment, at least) a person who walks past.

I've decided that I'd rather be someone who stoops to pick up the bottle, cup, or bag that is there. It feels better. And when I make that choice, I am moving toward becoming the person I want to be. Hopefully, that choice becomes a part of me in terms of my willingness, discipline, and self-concept. Those things become qualities that are less likely to shift suddenly if the discipline is practiced repeatedly. If the choice is healthy and positive, the results seem to carry over to other moments of my life and actions. Thus, the moment I pick up trash is a moment of investment that pays interest and dividends in the future—in the world, and in me.

A thought for today: I am free. How I use my freedom shows who I am and is creating who I will become.

Day Two

Thursday

Read John 18:28–37

Jesus answered, "You say that I am a king. For this I was born, and for this I came into the world, to testify to the truth. Everyone who belongs to the truth listens to my voice."

(John 18:37)

"Why should I clean up this mess? I wasn't the one who made it!"

That's one possible reaction to the trash I see, and I confess that even after years of trying to develop the "pick up the trash" habit, it's a reaction I feel from time to time.

Where does that reaction come from? Part of it comes from a sense of fairness and a sensible awareness of cause and effect. But part of it, I am sure, comes from inside me—the temptation to laziness and inaction that I know so well. Is it the voice of blame and condemnation that wants those who are guilty of making the mess to be held accountable? Or is it that tendency to not get involved, hoping that someone else—maybe those paid to do such things—will handle the problem?

I wonder if Jesus ever had those kinds of thoughts. Objections to having to deal with a messy, sinful world he didn't make that way would be reasonable for him. But Jesus seemed to hear another voice more clearly:

3

the one that called him to make a difference and to offer his life in cleaning up messy, sinful lives by freely sharing God's love and grace.

In John's account of Jesus before Pilate, Jesus says, "For this I was born, and for this I came into the world, to testify to the truth" (John 18:37). His mission had brought him to a place of pain, condemnation, and rejection. And yet he remained true to his mission. He wasn't the cause of the problems, but he offered his life as its solution.

As we begin the season of Lent, we're likely to see lots of trash around us—in our world, in others, and in ourselves. This spiritual season calls us to reflect, to repent, and to return to God. Do we *have* to get involved and do something to address the problems, needs, and failures we see? No. But Jesus's example and his invitation to follow him beckon us with the promise of purpose, change, and salvation if we do.

A thought for today: What "messy situations" are close enough that you could do something to help them?

Day Three

Friday

Read John 9:1–7

***As Jesus was walking along, he saw a man who had
been blind from birth. "Rabbi," his disciples asked
him, "why was this man born blind? Was it because
of his own sins or his parents' sins?"***

(John 9:1–2 NLT)

How did this get here?

It's not at all unusual for me to ask that question when I'm picking up
trash. A sock, a mitten, one shoe neatly placed by the side of the running
trail. Weird. Recently there were two very large "slushie" cups full of their
flavored—but now melted—contents (and complete with lids and straws)
tossed into my backyard. We don't drink slushies, and certainly not that
size! How did those get there?

Sometimes I'm simply curious. One shoe? What happened to the other one? But in the case of the slushie cup, I wanted to assign blame. Who
threw that over the fence into my yard?

Many of us are in the habit of asking *How did that get there?* about
what we read in the Bible, beginning at the outset. Consider the legitimate
questions we ask about Adam and Eve in the Garden of Eden. It's such
a fascinating story and provides some people with a way to point blame:

"If it weren't for Eve, everything would be perfect!" Our better scholars, however, tell us that the story is an etiological one. It's told to explain how things got the way they are, but at best it only describes that which is beyond our knowledge and which we probably don't need to know, even if we could fathom the answers. Why did God put that tree there? Why was the serpent placed there? Did the serpent really put the idea into the woman's head or just awaken something inherent in her human nature?

In my role as a pastor, it is sometimes important that I learn about the experiences, both good and bad, that have shaped my parishioners' lives. In counseling situations, it often becomes clear that there are guilty parties that have caused harm and left deep emotional scars in the lives of others. But much more often, the important thing is to simply note who and how they are and to accept them where they are. Like Jesus healing the blind man, I may be given the opportunity to help that person. And if that happens, perhaps the power of God will be seen. Regardless of how it got there, maybe I can help.

> *A thought for today: Sometimes it doesn't matter how the problem got there. The question is, "Is there something I can do about it?"*

Day Four

Saturday

Read Matthew 10:1–16

***See, I am sending you out like sheep into the midst of
wolves; so be wise as serpents and innocent as doves.***

(Matthew 10:16)

My run was shortened a bit because I hadn't dressed appropriately for
the cold and windy weather. I thought the warmth generated by my body
would take care of the chill, but I'd neglected to bring a hat or gloves, as
I should have. In most cases, it's better to have it and not need it than to
need it and not have it. I should have brought them.

Why I focused on the sheet of ruled notebook paper I don't know.
There's a middle school just a few blocks from my house, and I confess
I take a special interest in picking up trash that appears school-related.
On several occasions, what I've found had a name on it and seemed
important enough that I've taken it to the school, asking that the office
return it to a kid who I hope will be grateful to get her or his homework
back.

As I reached toward this particular piece of paper, however, a gust of
wind lifted it slightly and blew it about twenty feet away. I walked toward
the paper again, only to have it once again blow on down the alley. Not
to be thwarted, this time I jogged after it. But sure enough, it once again

escaped my grasp. Only when I'd followed it for almost a block did I realize I was now shivering from the cold. The paper continued to blow farther down the alley. I turned and headed home.

There have been times when I did the same sort of thing in trying to help someone who wasn't willing or ready to be helped. There have been times when I spent a disproportionate amount of time, energy, and money trying to improve a situation, only to realize in the end that I lacked the resources to do what I thought ought to be done. Perhaps that's why Jesus encouraged his disciples to be "wise as serpents, and gentle as doves." Some situations are simply not worth the cost to our spiritual or relational health. He said he was sending them out like sheep among wolves. Being able to recognize the wolves—whether they be persons or situations—that threaten our serenity or that are built upon an inflated sense of our own abilities is an important quality. Sheep generally don't stand a chance against wolves. Sometimes you have to just let things go.

A thought for today: If I am motivated by love and guided by wisdom, I'll better know what to do—and not to do.

First Sunday of Lent

Read Exodus 20:8–11

Remember the Sabbath day by keeping it holy. Six days you shall labor and do all your work, but the seventh day is a sabbath to the L<small>ORD</small> your God. On it you shall not do any work, neither you, nor your son or daughter, nor your male or female servant, nor your animals, nor any foreigner residing in your towns.

(Exodus 20:8–10 NIV)

Most days when I head out to run, I have a pretty good idea of my schedule for the next few hours. *Today is a fifty-minute run, then a fifteen-minute walk home, and then thirty minutes' yard work* (there's always something to be done there, and I like to tackle it while I'm already sweaty...), *leaving twenty minutes to get showered and dressed and twelve minutes for the drive to work, and the first thing to deal with when I get there is...*

There are some days the trash would lead me on and on down the street (and probably out into the countryside) if I just walked to the next piece I saw in the distance. There are days I have two hands full of cans and cups already when I come upon something that I'd like to pick up—but I don't have room among my fingers. Occasionally I'll go back and pick it up if I can get rid of what I've already collected in a nearby Dumpster or trashcan. But usually I don't go back. I don't have time, and there are days I don't have the energy. At those moments, I need to remember that it's okay if I don't accomplish everything all at once. Time spent on other things, even rest and relaxation on my days off from work, is also important. Steady commitment seems to be better than sporadic flurries of activity.

Today is a day of rest. Jesus spent time alone in prayer and on one occasion was either so tired or so much at peace that he was able to fall asleep on board a boat being rocked by a storm. I need to learn from his example in so many ways, and this is one of them. The Bible tells us that one day in six should be special and free from work. Today is that day, the Sabbath.

Many of us know that Lent is "the forty days before Easter." But if we count the total number of days between Ash Wednesday and Easter Sunday, we'll find that there are actually forty-six. The reason for this discrepancy is that Sundays aren't counted in the forty days of penance. Rather, they are to be celebrated in commemoration of the resurrection of Jesus. It's as if we are saying, "Yes, there are problems, and yes there is work to be done. No, the Kingdom is not yet here in its fullness. But the victory is already won. We don't have to do it all, just what we can, and according to God's leading. Salvation is not earned; it is given because of God's grace. It will be okay. Surely I can take a day off to rest, praise, and relax. God's in charge."

On the Sabbath, I will rest and trust.

A thought for today: The Sabbath is a day of rest, worship, and trust.

Monday

Read Luke 19:15–16

People were bringing even infants to him that he might touch them; and when the disciples saw it, they sternly ordered them not to do it. But Jesus called for them and said, "Let the little children come to me, and do not stop them; for it is to such as these that the kingdom of God belongs."

(Luke 19:15–16)

My picking-up-trash habit has carried over to moments other than my end-of-run cooldowns. If it's on my way, and if I can, I'll often pick up other pieces I see—on the way into an office building or store, on my way to or from a parking lot, even going into someone's home. I've never had anyone become upset that I picked up a piece of trash from their lawn, even if I'm bringing it into their house!

This morning I went to the store early for some dog food, since we had run out. I got a good parking place, right next to the cart-return spot, since I knew I would need one for the fifty-pound bag I was planning to buy. In the cart-return area, there was a trash receptacle that was less than three feet from my car door. When I opened my car door, my foot landed right beside a wadded-up bag from the fast-food joint across the road. I looked at the bag and then at the trash can. They were less than two feet from each other. It would have been so easy to put the trash into the trash can!

Sometimes the opportunities that come our way to live our Christian faith are like that image. They're right there—it just takes a small effort to do the little extra thing that would transform the situation. A smile, a nod, stopping for a moment to listen, or giving a sincere compliment. They're not difficult to do. The problem is that they're also easy *not* to do.

One of the most beloved images of the gospels is Jesus welcoming the little children. It doesn't say he preached to them or began thinking of a lesson series for them. It says he touched them. I imagine him smiling, perhaps patting them on their heads or backs—a simple gesture that somehow reminds us to not miss such moments of opportunity in our own lives.

A thought for today: Lord, help me notice the little, easy things I can do to help your creation become better.

Tuesday

Read Joel 2:1–2, 12–17

*That is why the L*ORD* says,*
"Turn to me now, while there is time.
Give me your hearts.
Come with fasting, weeping, and mourning.
Don't tear your clothing in your grief,
but tear your hearts instead."

(Joel 2:12–13 NLT)

I've mentioned the three reasons I feel compelled to pick up trash (I'm there, I can, it seems like the right thing to do.) There's also a fourth reason, though it's difficult to describe. Something inside me knows *I need to…or else.*

When I think, *I need to…or else,* it's not as if I fear some sort of punishment from without. It's more like a fear of what will transpire within (and then around) me if I don't. I've seen what's happened in my own life when I begin to let down in doing what I should. I've seen it in others as well. We push the limits of what we allow just a little, rationalizing time after time until what shouldn't be tolerated becomes something we accept without question. Drink a little more, year after year; don't read or exercise as much; stop attending church or reading the scriptures…after a time, we grow used to the new normal, even if it's not a healthy one. Like weeds creeping into even the most beautiful of lawns, simple neglect eventually leads to a mess that feels unconquerable.

Lent is a time to return to God. It's interesting that even nonliturgical churches have discovered the importance of this holy time of year, with many of them observing Lent in their churches even if they don't celebrate other liturgical seasons. There's something universal in our need to notice where we've strayed and return to God. We know it, we feel it. Let's not fear to turn around. Our gracious God awaits and will receive us yet again.

A thought for today: In what ways have I drifted away from where I sense God would have me be?

Wednesday

Read Mark 5:25–34

*A woman in the crowd had suffered for twelve years
with constant bleeding. She had suffered a great deal
from many doctors, and over the years she had spent
everything she had to pay them, but she had gotten
no better. In fact, she had gotten worse.*

(Mark 5:25–26 NLT)

Today I worked out at the YMCA—a forty-five-minute swim followed by a little while in the dry sauna. That was where I found an automobile magazine that had been left on the upper deck of seats. When I reached over to pick the magazine up, I found that it was no longer a magazine— rather, it was a stack of formerly bound together pages, all in order but no longer joined. I suppose the heat of the sauna had caused the binding adhesive to fail. I removed the stack of paper when I left the sauna, but my guess is it won't stay on the shelf where I left it for long. Someone will pitch it.

I wonder how many individuals who are suffering in one way or another would want us to know, "I wasn't always this way." The sadness of bereavement, the despair of grinding poverty, the wear and tear of physical disease, the stresses of homelessness, even the blessing of growing old all take their toll. We may see someone who seems feeble or whose life has seemingly come undone but surely that's not all that ought to be said about him or her.

A certain woman is described in all three synoptic gospels as someone who "had suffered for twelve years with constant bleeding." I'm sure there was more to her life and identity than this, but over time, she had become defined—at least in the eyes of others—by her condition.

This woman, however, had something else going for her—a daring, desperate faith in the power of Jesus to heal her. And because she dared to reach out to him, she was made well.

> ***A thought for today: Lord, help me see others as you see them. And may I, too, have desperate hope in your ability to help and heal us all.***

Thursday

Read Matthew 28:16–20

Therefore, go and make disciples of all the nations,
baptizing them in the name of the Father and the Son
and the Holy Spirit. Teach these new disciples to obey
all the commands I have given you. And be sure of
this: I am with you always, even to the end of the age.

(Matthew 28:19–20 NLT)

Today I ran on the recreational path that winds through our community. Much of the path is situated near a river, so at several spots along the way, I can note the water's height and flow.

The spring rains haven't yet begun, so the water is getting a little low—so low, in fact, that some unsightly debris is now exposed. What looks to be an old mattress (now little more than a rusty, rectangular arrangement of springs), along with an upside-down two-person rowboat are now peeking from the water. To me, they've made a beautiful scene into one that's ugly and embarrassing.

I don't have a way to go down there and pull those things out. I would need someone with a winch, a trailer, and a place to dump them. I'd probably have to check with the scenic rivers authority and ask if I could even try. I'm sure the police or parks department would like to know if someone was going to attempt such a project. And who owns the land on that side of the river? They'd need to grant access and perhaps unlock a gate or two.

Some of the things we'd like to see improved are like that. They're so big or longstanding that in order to tackle them we would need to come up with a plan and get some help from others. We may even have to plot and scheme and be patient in our approach in order to accomplish the good we seek.

Maybe that's why Jesus told his disciples that he was counting on their help. This saving-the-world business is so big and important that it needs to be carried out in every place and in every generation by as many as possible. Like him, I hope I won't be limited by the size of what needs to be done. After all, he's given us one another and promised to be with us in the tasks to which we're called.

A thought for today: Let's not be discouraged from doing what's needed just because it will take effort, planning, or resources. Big tasks often bring big rewards.

Friday

Read Romans 15:1–2

We who are strong ought to put up with the failings of the weak, and not to please ourselves. Each of us must please our neighbor for the good purpose of building up the neighbor.

(Romans 15:1–2)

One day, I was nearing my own driveway after my run, carrying a handful of trash. A car pulled past me and stopped at the stop sign, and the passenger in the front seat tossed out a cup. I was just a few yards away from them and had the strong urge to yell, "Hey!" In the tone I envisioned using, that one word would be enough—they'd know exactly what I was yelling about and how I felt about what he had done.

And then I realized that this person wasn't throwing out trash because I was there. He was oblivious to me and what I was doing. He was simply someone who throws trash out. My plan to yell in anger softened to a "doggone it" look of resignation on my face as the car drove off.

Although I've been hurt by others' words and actions many times in my life, only rarely has someone intended harm. In most cases, they're simply doing what they were taught or learned by example from others.

My experience is that most people do the best they can until they learn better.

The apostle Paul wrote in several places about "those who are weak"—whether in their faith, in their understanding, or in their ability to live a disciplined life. He encourages being patient with others' shortcomings for the sake of establishing a relationship with them through which we might help them learn a better way. While I might be tempted to immediately correct or shame someone when he or she does something of which I do not approve, it's usually better to believe that the person is probably doing the best he or she can at this moment in time. Maybe if I'm patient and kind, I'll be given the opportunity to help him or her learn a better way.

> **A thought for today: Most people are doing the best they can. Remembering this can help us practice patience.**

Saturday

Read Philippians 2:1–11

***Don't look out only for your own interests, but take
an interest in others, too.***

(Philippians 2:4 NLT)

One of the routes I run ends near downtown. On the half-mile or so walk home, I can walk right past our church's property, which shares an alley-way with the Presbyterian Church next door (a fine congregation made up of some wonderful Christian people).

One day, I was walking through the alley, where both churches have their Dumpsters. Right in the middle of the alley sat some large, empty boxes. I assumed they'd been placed beside either their Dumpsters or ours, by either their custodial staff or our own, and that the wind had re-located them to this neutral site. But whose were they?

And then I realized that it didn't really matter. It was our alley, together. I decided that I would put the boxes into our Dumpster if there was room, but if not, I'd use theirs and feel okay about it.

There are times when I hear of human need in far-off places. Sometimes it's in another city or state; sometimes in a different country on a faraway continent. It's true that I may not be able to do much about those problems, especially since some seem so intractable and chronic. But I should at least care, since we inhabit the same earth.

Dr. Martin Luther King Jr. said, "Injustice anywhere is a threat to justice everywhere." In the same manner, goodness practiced anywhere is a benefit to goodness everywhere. May God help me care about the needs of others, wherever they may be.

> *A thought for today: When we care, help, give, and share, everyone benefits.*

Second Sunday of Lent

Read Mark 2:23–27

Then he said to them, "The sabbath was made for humankind, and not humankind for the sabbath."

(Mark 2:27)

I work out six days a week but never on Sundays. One reason is because I'm a pastor and am usually at the church well before sunup on Sundays. The other is that some years ago I read that the difference between working out five days versus seven is negligible in terms of benefit to the body, and you risk injury or overuse by working out every day of the week. Whether that is absolutely true or not, I don't know. But I like it, so I live by it.

On more than one occasion, Jesus was taken to task for doing what was not lawful, in terms of proper Sabbath behavior. On the occasion described in Mark's gospel, he counters his critics by saying, in effect, "Hey, lay off! People need to eat!"

I wonder how many times I have been less than holy precisely because I was trying so hard to be holy, working and worrying for God's sake. When I work all the time, I'm more likely to show the stress in curt or unkind remarks, in a "can't you see how hard I'm working" type attitude, or as a friend of mine put it, playing "dueling martyrs" with anyone who complains about his or her difficult and overburdened life.

The Sabbath is given to us not as a way of rigidly obeying rules, whether they be about working or not working. It's simply a day to rest, relax, and do what is needed so that we are properly fed—spiritually, emotionally, relationally, and physically.

> *A thought for today: If the way I spend my Sabbath is not making me stronger and better, I'm doing something wrong.*

Monday

Read Psalm 104

He sends forth springs in the valleys;
They flow between the mountains;
They give drink to every beast of the field;
The wild donkeys quench their thirst.
Beside them the birds of the heavens dwell;
They lift up their voices among the branches.
He waters the mountains from His upper chambers;
The earth is satisfied with the fruit of His works.

(Psalm 104:10–13 NASB)

In addition to running, I'm also a cyclist. Getting off the bike to pick up trash is not usually an option the way it is while walking home at the end of my run, but what's thrown along the road and encountered while cycling also provides an opportunity for insight and conversation with God.

Take, for example, the difference between what's seen while cycling as opposed to driving. Because road cyclists like smooth pavement, my riding is done on streets, county roads, and even some highways where there is an adequate shoulder. When driving, my eyes are focused ahead while I try to remain aware of what's going on behind me by glancing in my rearview mirror at appropriate angles to the left and right. Because of the speed at which an automobile travels, it's the big things that are noticed: an entire field, the cars around me, the traffic up ahead. But when I'm cycling, I see so much more!

Ask almost any cyclist and he or she will tell you that there are some interesting things on and near roadways. Driving past, you wouldn't notice them; you're going too fast, and besides, you've got to focus on the road ahead and the cars nearby. Getting where I want to arrive as soon as possible and hopefully without hindrance is the focus when driving.

But cycling is slower. When on the bike, it's more about the ride itself. You see bugs walking, plants flowering, snakes slithering, coins (I've found coins on long stretches of highway or out in remote countryside roads nowhere near where someone would typically stop), bolts, tools, bungee cords, and all kinds of other interesting things. I simply would not have noticed these if driving my car on the same route. Going slower alters what you're able to notice.

Lent is an opportunity to slow down and notice both the good and bad around us and in us. God's good universe, God's Holy Spirit, and the life and teachings of Jesus are all wonderful things that God has given. But there's also the pollution of my own sin, complex economic and political problems, and the nagging persistence of religious intolerance, racial and ethnic animosities, and human greed. Am I seeing what needs to be noticed?

Sometimes I come back from a bike ride refreshed by the beauty I've experienced. Other times, I come back with a determination to clean up a portion of the roadside. Perhaps that's another lesson of Lent—to not allow this forty-day journey to pass without at least noticing what needs to be seen.

A thought for today: Today, I will pause to notice what's around me and inside me and will open myself to the one who has promised to be with me.

Tuesday

Read Luke 5:12–16

In one of the villages, Jesus met a man with an advanced case of leprosy. When the man saw Jesus, he bowed with his face to the ground, begging to be healed. "Lord," he said, "if you are willing, you can heal me and make me clean."
Jesus reached out and touched him. "I am willing," he said. "Be healed!" And instantly the leprosy disappeared.

(Luke 5:12–13 NLT)

"This is gross."

There is some trash I'm not crazy about picking up. Used disposable diapers people have thrown out, cups with syrupy soda with swarming ants, and wet paper (even though it's probably wet from merely rain or dew) all cause me to react with a "Yuck! I don't want to touch that!" And chances are you wouldn't want to either.

The gospels tell us Jesus went around touching people who were considered "yucky" by others. There were those who were ceremonially unclean, those who were unclean because of their ethnicity, and even those who were diseased (and thus I suppose were in some ways dangerous to touch since they brought the risk of infection).

And yet he touched them.

When I see trash that is particularly gross and dirty, I try to recall that the grime and slime won't make me worse—it'll wash off. But not bending over to pick it up because I think I'm too good or too clean might do some damage to my soul. If I'm not willing to get a little dirty for the sake of cleaning up my neighborhood, I've become part of the problem. If I worry that someone might see me carrying a dirty diaper a few steps and think worse of me, I've given in to a problem that continues to plague humanity: fear of judgment that keeps us from reaching out to others who in some cases are not clean, may not be considered "proper," or are disenfranchised in some manner or another.

A thought for today: Which is a greater danger to you and your discipleship: getting involved in the dirty, yucky problems around you, or avoiding them?

Day Thirteen

Wednesday

Read Luke 3:7–15

*The crowd asked him (John), "Then what are we
supposed to do?"
"If you have two coats, give one away," he said. "Do
the same with your food."*

(Luke 3:10–11 MSG)

It was a wadded-up burger sack, and it appeared as if someone had pitched it out while driving down the street. The last bite or two of the sandwich itself was lying about six inches from the sack. The whole mess was perched on a nicely mowed lawn, so I decided to pick up the food too.

When I was about six feet away, almost ready to begin reaching down toward the sack, a mockingbird came swooping down and landed right beside it. Its posture seemed defiant: tail feathers angled upward, chest puffed. The bird looked at me briefly, grabbed the hamburger bun in its beak and flew away. All I was able to do was stop, straighten up and marvel at the bird's audacity.

What I figured as trash and waste—good for only the bin—was something better in the eyes of that flying opportunist. As I continued on toward home, I couldn't help but wonder about the other resources I view as disposable but that might be of use to others in God's creation. I thought about the crowded coat closet in our downstairs hallway, filled with some coats and jackets that we haven't worn in well over a year. I can't imagine someone coming boldly to our door to claim what we could share, but maybe it would be good if they did.

John the baptizer would have a problem with our coat closet. I can't help but think that Jesus would too. And now that I've begun to notice it, so do I. I should swoop in and take some away to share with others in need. I hope I'll be as bold as that bird in doing so.

A thought for today: What am I not using that I could share with someone else?

Thursday

Read Genesis 2:1–25

**The LORD God placed the man in the Garden of Eden
to tend and watch over it.**

(Genesis 2:15 NLT)

I clearly recall how struck I was the first time I heard the phrase as a participant in a Bible studies series. I'd been studying the scriptures for years, had been to seminary, and had become an ordained minister, and yet I had never heard it before. It jolted me by its audacity and truth: "We are cocreators with God."

It was used to describe the role and powers given to human beings, as those called to work with God in the act of creation. I could not avoid the implied responsibility and fearful truth of the words. We *are* cocreators with God.

Of course, much of what we create is not so good. In ignorance, shortsightedness, or downright wickedness, we shape the world in ways that are not pleasing to God and not good for humanity. How different might things be if we truly saw ourselves as "working for God" in the continuing work of creation?

The first thing the Bible says about humanity's role and function is that "the man was placed in the Garden of Eden to tend and watch over it" (Genesis 2:15). There's no way that we can escape responsibility for the many ways we have polluted, used up, and even ruined portions of the world God has placed into our hands. That's why I believe that picking up trash is somehow quite close to one of the best, humblest, and most appropriate things we can do in fulfilling our given role as created beings.

> *A thought for today: I am put here to help God's continued work of creation.*

Friday

Read Hebrews 12:1–3

Therefore, since we are surrounded by such a huge crowd of witnesses to the life of faith, let us strip off every weight that slows us down, especially the sin that so easily trips us up. And let us run with endurance the race God has set before us.

(Hebrews 12:1–2 NLT)

One of the reasons I wanted to write about my trash habit is to encourage others to "pick up" the habit (pun intended). If just one other person did the same amount of cleaning up as I do, the effect would be doubled. But I like thinking bigger, because making a bigger difference is so within reach (pun intended again).

Let's say, for the sake of argument (and in order to keep the math easy) that I pick up 1 piece of trash in our community five days a week. Five days times fifty-two weeks equals 260 pieces of trash. Maybe not all that impressive, but the place is 260 pieces cleaner than if I didn't!

But I preach to several hundred people each Sunday, with a few hundred more who follow our Facebook page and a few hundred more who watch the local broadcast of our worship services on television. So let's say (again, as a way of keeping the math easy) that I was able to convince a thousand of these people to join me in the effort. One thousand a day times five weekdays equals five thousand a week. Five thousand each week times fifty-two weeks in the year means our town is 260,000 pieces cleaner each year. Now we're talking!

And what did it cost? Just the effort of one piece of trash a day (or for those who prefer, five pieces one day each week) shared by some like-minded people who committed themselves to the cause.

No wonder the Bible speaks time and again of the encouragement we receive through being part of the community of faith. There's power there: the ability to persuade, join in, invite others, and do God's will in all kinds of ways.

> *A thought for today: Thank God for those who stay strong when we cannot; thank God for the ability to be strong when others cannot; and thank God for those marvelous moments when we are all strong together.*

Saturday

Read John 4:1–30

The woman was surprised, for Jews refuse to have anything to do with Samaritans. She said to Jesus, "You are a Jew, and I am a Samaritan woman. Why are you asking me for a drink?"

(John 4:9 NLT)

Today was another bike riding day. While on my ride, I saw a couple of bolts, a pair of pliers, and a bungee cord along my way. The pliers I put beside a nearby mailbox. Maybe the owner of the house can use them. The bungee cord I stuffed in the back pouch of my cycling jersey to add to the collection at home.

Spotting these things (and knowing I would miss them if I had been driving the same route) makes me think about the ways in which I am so often in a hurry in other ways, no doubt missing lots of interesting and perhaps important things along the way.

I am often guilty of realizing too late that a short and hurried conversation with someone was actually an opportunity to notice and explore something that I moved past too quickly. The person who says "I'm fine" but whose face sends a different message or the child who begins an excited, stuttering explanation that I fail to tease out and fully understand are the kinds of situations that I would do better to approach at a less hurried pace.

In that famous story we love to tell, Jesus had time for children. He spent time on an extended conversation with a Samaritan woman at a well, who seemed surprised by his attention. In several stories from the gospels, we see that while he was doing his father's business, he took time to teach and then to explain parables when needed.

When I'm focused solely on my own objectives and on getting to where I want to go, I miss seeing so much along the way! The world and its people are so interesting and beautiful.

> **A thought for today: Today, I'll move at a pace that allows me to see, enjoy, and explore more fully.**

Third Sunday in Lent

Read Matthew 17:14–20

Truly I tell you, if you have faith the size of a mustard seed, you will say to this mountain, "Move from here to there," and it will move; and nothing will be impossible for you.

(Matthew 17:20)

Years ago, Georgia and I and our then only child, Paige, lived in Ireland. I counted it our good fortune to be stationed in a small seaside village, amid miles and miles of rugged but well-tended farmland. Along with small thatched-roof cottages, castle ruins, and hillsides filled with sheep, we resided near many examples of another classic Irish scene: precisely partitioned fields and farms, separated by walls of beautifully stacked stone.

Seeing kilometer after kilometer of these boundaries, it's easy to wonder, "Where did they get all these rocks?" The answer, of course, is that they came from the fields themselves and were slowly built over generations. Whenever a new rock is found, it's fitted into place somewhere along the boundary.

Perhaps that's the kind of miracle Jesus had in mind when he said that faith—even if it's small as a mustard seed—can move mountains. I've known people who were in and out of addiction recovery several times and then, because they dared to believe sobriety could happen, they tried once more…and got sober. It's a miracle. I've known people whose staunch but unpromising chemotherapy treatments kept them alive until a better protocol came along and put their cancer into remission. And I've struggled with sin in my own life in ways that seemed chronic; my only hope is having enough faith to keep opening myself to the Master's touch.

I don't pick up trash expecting the problem to be quickly fixed, because having faith to keep on trying is more important than reaching the goal. Some tasks are so awesome in scope and scale that they make us want to give up and give in. Faith doesn't let us do so, even if the problem is bigger than us and the project longer than our lifetimes. Faith, after all, sees what our eyes cannot. And faith well placed is not planted in our own abilities but in God's.

Today, I will remember that whether it's a struggle against rocks, sin, trash, or despair, I only need enough to let God keep on touching me. Eventually, I will be made whole in God's presence.

A thought for today: Just having faith to reach out toward God is enough to work miracles.

Day Seventeen

Monday

Read Genesis 1:1–2:3

***Then God looked over all he had made, and he saw
that it was very good!***

(Genesis 1:31 NLT)

Today's run was glorious. Yesterday was a rest day, so I had more energy
than usual. The weather was perfect: low- to midsixties, no wind. But best
of all was the fact that signs of spring's pending arrival were on display:
trees budding, a few flowers blooming, spots of green beginning to appear in the lawns and fields. I could just sense that at a molecular level
something was waiting to happen in the world.

At the end of my run, I sat down on a bench in the park. Right beside
the bench was today's trash, almost as if it had been placed there for me.
I reached down to pick it up, and when I did, I noticed motion underneath.
Tiny bugs were scurrying around, no doubt doing whatever tiny bugs are
supposed to be doing at this time of year. *Cool,* I thought. I just saw the
trash at first, but there was better and more interesting stuff underneath.

Many expositors have noted that in the biblical account of creation,
God declares each thing created to be good until the creation of human
beings. At that point, the creation is said to be "very good."

I believe in the goodness and potentiality of humanity. I am also aware of the sin and wickedness that has marred the divine image in us. I sense it in myself: if I could but allow God to fully remove those negative aspects of my being, something good lies underneath. I can't seem to do it on my own. I need God to remove those things. The good news is that's what God offers to do.

A thought for today: Underneath the trash in my life is something God has made and declared very good.

Tuesday

Read Matthew 6:1–6, 16–21

So whenever you give alms, do not sound a trumpet before you, as the hypocrites do in the synagogues and in the streets, so that they may be praised by others. Truly I tell you, they have received their reward.

(Matthew 6:2)

I've told my congregation about my trash habit. One reason is as a proactive defense against any misunderstanding that might lead to gossip. If the preacher is spotted coming home some morning looking a bit worn and carrying what appears to be a pack of smokes and an empty fifth, I want them to know what's going on!

I must confess, however, that a part of me would like to be spotted doing this trash thing so that they'll appreciate me. Is that wrong? Jesus said we shouldn't seek recognition for the good things we do. Does that mean I should suddenly hide the Marlboros and Michelob behind my back? Seems like that might be asking for trouble.

I think Jesus was pointing us toward deeper dimensions of doing good and how doing good for the sake of its intrinsic rightness is better and more satisfying than doing it for the sake of others' approval. And when we do what's right for the sake of our own devotion to God, we don't require an audience of others. The One who sees and knows is enough.

> *A thought for today: God sees, and God knows. May my actions bring me satisfaction, and may they bring God joy.*

Day Nineteen

Wednesday

Read Matthew 5:13–16

No one lights a lamp and then puts it under a basket. Instead, a lamp is placed on a stand, where it gives light to everyone in the house. In the same way, let your good deeds shine out for all to see, so that everyone will praise your heavenly Father.

(Matthew 5:15–16 NLT)

Yes, I confess again today that I enjoy having others see me picking up the trash. They don't have to be people I know, and they don't have to recognize me. I'd just like for them to see me doing this good thing. Maybe they'll be inspired to try it too. I know I feel encouraged when I see or hear of people helping or serving in meaningful ways, whether large or small. Maybe this small action of mine might provide encouragement to whatever their calling is.

Hearing what Jesus had to say about "letting your good deeds shine" gives me some perspective on this whole affair, especially when held in proper tension with his warning about wanting to be praised by others (Matthew 6). It's the motivation that matters.

Showing off so that others will see is something that depends upon having an audience. A sincere desire to help others see and sense the joy and goodness of being part of God's work is quite another matter. That's a kind of being seen that can bless them, those they touch, and all those to whom it spreads.

> *A thought for today: We can be happy and proud about being found doing the right things for the right reasons.*

Thursday

Read John 6:60–69

***At this point many of his disciples turned away and
deserted him. Then Jesus turned to the Twelve and
asked, "Are you also going to leave?"***

(John 6:66 NLT)

We are halfway through the forty days of Lent. There are doubtless those who have already given up on their Lenten disciplines and others for whom the temptation to do so is very real. I understand what that's like: there have been years when I failed to follow through on my intentions for Lent and other years when I was sorely tempted to do so...both by rationalizations from within and by circumstances without.

Not every good thing we intend to do—whether picking up trash or writing notes or seeking reconciliation with another—is always faithfully accomplished in the way we originally planned. Sometimes we'll just need to start over and try again later. At other times, one type of person is separated from others—those who are able to deal with hard things and those who are not. The very season of Lent itself is based upon the reality that most of us drift away from God over time and need an intentional time of return and recommitment.

Kevin Tully

Jesus dealt with the fact that many can't seem to stay on course. I suspect he probably felt disappointed by those who dropped out in response to some teachings that offended them. We're told that on at least one occasion in his ministry, "many of his disciples turned away and deserted him." Most of us will be on both sides of that equation at various moments in our lives. We will know the pain of having others let us down, perhaps even turning against us. We will also likely be among those who have at times drawn back from the difficult parts of faithful discipleship: faithful tithing, forgiving and praying for our enemies, denying ourselves, and taking up the way of the cross.

Jesus said that fully accepting him, through the power of the Holy Spirit, was what makes the difference. When Jesus asked of the Twelve—perhaps rhetorically, in painful disappointment—if they too would leave, Simon Peter answered, "Lord, to whom would we go? You have the words that give eternal life."

In those moments when we are tempted to give up, give in, or draw back, perhaps we will remember that in Jesus there is strength, forgiveness, and reward at the end of the journey. Hang in there.

A thought for today: Lord, help me stay the course even when the way is difficult. Send your Holy Spirit's power when mine is insufficient.

Friday

Read Luke 9:21–27

Then he said to the crowd, "If any of you wants to be my follower, you must give up your own way, take up your cross daily, and follow me. If you try to hang on to your life, you will lose it. But if you give up your life for my sake, you will save it. And what do you benefit if you gain the whole world but are yourself lost or destroyed?"

(Luke 9:23–25 NLT)

My children are the most precious beings in the world to me. One day, when my daughter was just a few months old, I was lifting her and her carrier out of the car, preparing to go into a store. I was young and strong, so I held the carrier in one hand along with my car keys and reached back into the car to get a cup of coffee I was drinking. Somehow, I lost my grip on the carrier, and it slipped from my hand. My darling daughter—my only daughter—fell to the street with a thud. Fortunately, the carrier dropped straight down, landing on its bottom. She was startled and cried, but she wasn't hurt. I, however, was completely shaken. I began to tremble, and then to cry, as I knelt down beside her, saying to this three-month-old, "Oh, Paigey, Paigey…I'm sorry! I'm sorry! I'm so sorry!"

I've thought about that incident for more than thirty years now. Those keys, that coffee—they could not compare with the value of what lay within that baby carrier. And yet, there I was, trying to juggle them along with something—and someone—that should have occupied my full and undivided attention.

Somehow, the call of Jesus to "take up our cross daily" is at the heart of Lent. I can't explain it all, and I don't yet understand it fully, but my soul somehow knows that it is undivided obedience and faithful attention to our Lord's teaching that is far superior to anything else. And yet, I spend so much time and attention on things that are inane, shallow, and short-lived. As the apostle Paul wrote, all that other stuff is garbage when compared to Christ (Philippians 3:8). There are times when hanging onto those other things leads to disaster. At the very least, they keep us from experiencing the fullness of meaning that following Christ can bring. Today, may I see clearly what holds most importance and give full attention to his call and claim on me.

A thought for today: Nothing is more important than holding onto the Lord.

Saturday

Read Matthew 5:21–30

So when you are offering your gift at the altar, if you remember that your brother or sister has something against you, leave your gift there before the altar and go; first be reconciled to your brother or sister, and then come and offer your gift. Come to terms quickly with your accuser while you are on the way to court with him, or your accuser may hand you over to the judge, and the judge to the guard, and you will be thrown into prison. Truly I tell you, you will never get out until you have paid the last penny.

(Matthew 5:23–26)

For some reason, I encountered more than the usual amount of trash yesterday. Not only that, but the pieces were larger than average: a shoe box (no top), a jumbo-sized Styrofoam drink cup, several straws, a few soft drink cans, and a beer bottle. In fact, I became a bit obsessed with how much I was collecting and paused to shuffle and shift the pieces into a more manageable arrangement. I put the straws into the bottle, the bottle into the cup, the cup into the shoe box, and so on. I kept picking up more. I once again paused to rearrange things into a manageable system. After another block, I was now carrying a larger box, into which the shoe box could fit. I was a little proud of how much I'd garnered. My only regret was the fact that others couldn't see how much I was carrying, since it appeared I was only carrying the large box.

I looked up ahead, and there was the trash truck, emptying my neighborhood's trash containers. I walked a bit faster, since the truck and I were coming from different directions and I hoped to make it to my trash container first, depositing everything in time to have it taken away. I thought, *Who knows? I may even be able to time it so that at least the trash crew will be impressed with how much I picked up.*

I paused a few more times to pick up a few more bits, arranging them in the box. But now, the trash truck was already at my driveway, and I was almost a half-block away. I missed my chance. Sure, they'd be back next week, but if I hadn't been so busy trying to win my little internal contest, I could have gotten it on board the hauler today.

Later, I thought of times in my life when I had been so concerned with carrying around weighty and sometimes ugly things that I missed opportunities to let them go in a timely fashion. Times I should have cleared the air of tension between another person and me. Times I didn't act on duties or decisions I was dreading undertaking, only to later find that not doing them weighed me down more and sometimes caused me days of stress when just addressing them would have been the smarter thing to do.

No wonder Jesus spoke of taking care of such matters as soon as we think of them. When we let go of the guilt, regret, or fear that are so often associated with difficulties in relationships, we not only keep those troubles from festering further, we also find ourselves freed from the mental and spiritual energies required to carry them around.

A thought for today: Lord, help me become aware of the things I'm carrying in my head and heart that are weighing me down. Help me do what I can to let them go and to entrust them into your merciful care.

Fourth Sunday in Lent

Read Matthew 11:28–30

Then Jesus said, "Come to me, all of you who are weary and carry heavy burdens, and I will give you rest. Take my yoke upon you. Let me teach you, because I am humble and gentle at heart, and you will find rest for your souls. For my yoke is easy to bear, and the burden I give you is light."

(Matthew 11:28–30 NLT)

Our neighborhood has a weekly trash pickup day. I sometimes put the trash bin by the curb the night before, but just as often I rise early to roll it down the driveway and leave it there. There have been times when I forget to do so, and when that happens, the next week may be a bit of a strain. We're not equipped to store up two weeks of our typical accumulation.

We pay for our trash service, but it's such a bargain! It requires only a little effort to leave it by the curb, and the trash truck comes by and does its thing. Upon arriving home in the evening, I walk to the end of the driveway, sometimes peek inside if the lid's closed, and think to myself, *Cool.*

Sunday is such a day for many of us. A time to get up a little early, if necessary, and go to worship. There, we have the opportunity to place the week's struggles, sins, and concerns before One who has the power to take them away and set us right for the week that is to come.

The coming days will no doubt bring an accumulation of the same sort of thing, but I'll once again have the opportunity to trust in the power of the gathered community of faith in singing, worship, silence, and confession. And when I do, I'll feel that I'm part of a gracious arrangement that is a blessing and a bargain. Driving home, I'll think, *Cool.*

> **A thought for today: We're not equipped for convenient storage of two weeks of a typical accumulation of life's ugly by-products. Better to get rid of it regularly every Sabbath.**

Day Twenty-Three

Monday

Read Jonah 3:1–4:11

*And should I not be concerned about Nineveh, that
great city, in which there are more than a hundred
and twenty thousand persons who do not know their
right hand from their left, and also many animals?*

(Jonah 4:11)

I'll admit the plant that I've been caring for does not look well. One after another, leaves and stalks have turned brown and died. Perhaps it's seasonal—after all, it is the end of winter. Perhaps it's the pot or the soil, or perhaps I haven't found a place where it can get enough sun.

My wife says throw it out, that we can get a new one. She's right in her assessment that it really does look bad. Even the beautiful pot it's in can't make it attractive. But I'm stubbornly caring for it, hoping it will survive and get better. There's just something about the fact that there are still signs of life that make it seem wrong to toss it. I don't want it to be trash.

Surely there's a lesson there for the way I regard others. Those who are old, obviously destitute, or challenged by some physical or mental condition should be cared for in the same way. They may be in their later years, or they may show signs of distress and sickness in their actions, but there's life there. They are children of God who ought to be treasured, nurtured, and given every chance to thrive.

The struggle to see as God sees—even those who are of different nationalities, ethnicities, and religions (as the Ninevites were in the story of Jonah)—is perhaps as old as human history itself. I hope I'll be as patient and determined in caring for them as I am my plant.

A thought for today: Where there is life, there is hope.

Day Twenty-Four

Tuesday

Read Luke 13:1–9

No, I tell you; but unless you repent,
you will all perish as they did.

(Luke 13:3)

There have been moments in my life when I believe I benefited from divine intervention. A doubter might say that I have attributed to God what was actually random chance. But no, I've seen it time and time again in my own life and in the lives of others. I know a little about statistical probability, and it's my sincere belief that God occasionally gets involved in an amazing and merciful way.

There are also times when I've cried out to God for help and mercy and didn't receive it...or at least, I didn't receive what I felt was needed. My faith was real and my need was desperate, but for whatever reasons, God didn't get involved the way I wanted. True, God didn't create the problem I hoped might be solved (I can take credit for most of those), but neither did God bail me out.

Because I'm a parent, I can understand how some of this might be seen from the divine perspective. There are times when my kids got more mercy from me and their mom than they deserved (but that makes sense because mercy is about not getting what we deserve). There were also times when I felt they needed to learn something that could only be taught through allowing the consequences of their actions to play out. In those cases, the most loving (in the long term) thing I could do was the thing that was also painful...for them and for me.

When it comes to the matter of trash—both the bits of litter in the neighborhood and the large-scale poisonings wrought by multinational corporations—I'm praying for merciful divine intervention but expecting hard lessons to come our way. There are many miraculous processes that God has already built into nature. (Dirt and rock filters nonpotable water into becoming clean again? We breathe out what trees breathe in, and they do the same for us? Dead matter is transformed into the stuff that's necessary for life? Amazing!) As we're told in the Genesis story of Eden, God's already done all the hard part of creation—we're just asked to help maintain the balance.

Will we learn, return, and repent? If we don't, we can expect disaster. If that happens, it won't be because God is sending special punishment. It will be due to our refusal to listen, learn, and change. And God will weep.

A thought for today: The earth and its systems can take only so much abuse. Praying for God's will to be done is only half the battle.

Wednesday

Read Luke 24:13–35

*And they said to one another, "Did not our heart
burn within us while He talked with us on the road,
and while He opened the Scriptures to us?" So they
rose up that very hour and returned to Jerusalem,
and found the eleven and those who were with them
gathered together, saying, "The Lord is risen indeed,
and has appeared to Simon!" And they told about the
things that had happened on the road, and how He
was known to them in the breaking of bread.*

(Luke 24:32–35 NKJV)

Lest I give the impression that I'm somehow extravirtuous because I pick
up trash, let me tell you about how and where the whole idea (for me,
anyway) got started.

Years ago, I was to be the luncheon guest of a bank president. We
would dine in the restaurant that sits near the top of his bank's building.
In other words, swanky.

He picked me up right on time, drove to the underground parking
garage under the bank building, and we got out and headed toward the
elevators. As we walked from his reserved space toward the glass doors,

he came to a small piece of paper on the ground. Without a word, he reached down to pick it up and carried it toward the trash bin. I jokingly said, "Don't you have people to do that for you?" He smiled kindly and said, "It's my job too."

It's difficult to describe the experience of what "burned within" me at that moment: embarrassment for my smug, condescending attitude and deep, inspired respect for his.

I cannot help but believe that our attitude and actions make a more profound impact upon those who join us on life's journey than we may suspect. My friend's simple gesture caused me to think, reflect, and then change. Luke says the risen Jesus was seen in the breaking of the bread at a house in Emmaus. But that "a-ha!" moment was set up by the time walking and talking on the way there. Ordinary activity—profound experience.

So much of our life's impact is done "on the way" to where we're going. Sometimes it's destructive—a lie, a broken promise, cheating, or gossiping. But with the Spirit's guidance, we can impact things constructively. Truth-telling, keeping our covenants, being generous, and treating others in the way we would want to be treated might just be noticed—and imitated—by those nearby.

A thought for today: Is there a little thing on the way to wherever you're headed that God would say is "your job too"?

Day Twenty-Six

Thursday

Read Matthew 5:38–48

If you are sued in court and your shirt is taken from you, give your coat, too. If a soldier demands that you carry his gear for a mile, carry it two miles. Give to those who ask, and don't turn away from those who want to borrow.

(Matthew 5:40–42)

I think (and hope) my trash habit is helping. But let's face it: I don't really go out of my way very much, and it rarely costs me much extra time. If you want to see someone who spends time and effort on stewardship of creation, look to my wife.

Georgia and I have been married since 1980. And somewhere along the way—probably earlier than I began picking up trash—she decided that our family ought to do our part at recycling. It's been interesting to live in several different cities during that time and to note the varying degrees of interest in recycling shown in each of them. There were times we lived somewhere that made it necessary for her to drive to the next town over in order to find a site that would take the stuff. But still, she did it. She was determined to make a difference, even if it was costly to do so.

Truth be told, she is the person in our family who makes this happen. The rest of us just toss our stuff in the bin. She sorts, organizes, drives it over, and unloads it faithfully each week. She's even taken others people's plastic, cardboard, and glass (sometimes carrying it around in her vehicle for a day or two) to the recycling center.

Isn't it true that the real difference-makers in life are those who do more than the minimum, more than average, and more than expected? Jesus's description of a world where people forgive, pray for their enemies, give more than they're asked, and put forth more effort than others is not just a hope; it's what will be required to get different results than the minimum, average, or expected. But isn't that what we hope for?

> *A thought for today: Instead of asking "What's the least I can do?" find a way to go the second mile. If you do, things will have changed already.*

Day Twenty-Seven

Friday

Read Colossians 3:1–17

*Since God chose you to be the holy people he loves,
you must clothe yourselves with tenderhearted
mercy, kindness, humility, gentleness, and patience.
Make allowance for each other's faults, and forgive anyone who offends you. Remember, the Lord
forgave you, so you must forgive others. Above all,
clothe yourselves with love, which binds us all together in perfect harmony.*

(Colossians 3:12–14 NLT)

Last year my congregation granted me a two-month sabbatical during the summer. Some thoughtful friends offered the use of their property in Crested Butte, Colorado, for one of those months. I gratefully said yes to their kind offer and spent a wonderful time there. I hiked, read, rested, painted, played guitar, rode my bike, attended church and some twelve-step meetings, and generally decompressed. Our dog Darby went with me, so we spent a lot of time together.

I brought back a painting of a sunset scene I did while there. It's not museum-quality, but it's not bad either. It currently hangs at the landing near the top of the stairs. It looks good from as far away as thirty feet and as close as four feet. Get much closer, however and you'll spot a curiosity.

There are lines of texture that seem not to fit what's painted. Little ridges of raised paint on the canvas seem almost to form a pattern. Look at it just right, and you'll see the truth: the ridges and bumps are in the shape of petals, stems, and leaves. The reason is that before it became a sunset, the canvas bore a bouquet of flowers.

Crested Butte is a funky town with its own vibe. One of the things I learned within the first week there is that rather than throw things away, many of the residents simply put whatever thing they're clearing out by their driveway with a sign that says Free. It could be an old bike, a hair dryer, or a waffle iron. There were sweaters, gloves and ski gear neatly folded and placed in boxes. Shoes. Boots. Kids' clothing. And the painting of the flowers was one such "free to anyone" offering.

Beauty is in the eye of the beholder, so it's impossible to declare my work on that canvas as superior to its first artist's. But the idea of taking something old and unwanted and adding some mental and creative energy to remake it into something new is, I think, a lesson in life. Today I'm especially thinking of friendships that may seem old and stale...or which we may be tempted to toss away. With a little ingenuity and effort, perhaps we can transform them into something that might beautify our environment for years and years. *"Above all, clothe yourselves with love, which binds us all together in perfect harmony."* Today, I'll try to beautify my relationships with the love of Christ.

> **A thought for today: God can help us see possibilities for beauty, love, and kindness.**

Day Twenty-Eight

Saturday

Read Luke 12:22–34

Sell your possessions, and give alms. Make purses for yourselves that do not wear out, an unfailing treasure in heaven, where no thief comes near and no moth destroys. For where your treasure is, there your heart will be also.

(Luke 12:33–34)

I have at least a dozen bungee cords in my garage, and I routinely give them away when helping someone pack and strap something onto their vehicle. "Keep it…I've got plenty," I say. The black, rubbery ones, the nylon and elastic ones with the bright colors, the long ones and short ones—I got 'em all. But guess what—I haven't purchased any sort of bungee cord for years. I just find them!

One thing about bungee cords—they're very flexible. While I'm on my bike rides, I may not be able to pick up the large bolt I think I might someday need, but bungee cords fold nicely to fit into my cycling jersey's rear pocket. And that's what I generally do when I come upon one.

Sometimes, when I stop to pick one up, I wonder about the cargo it was strapped to. Did it arrive safely? Were there backup straps of some sort? How did this particular cord come off—it obviously wasn't well secured, or it wouldn't be here.

Jesus spoke some very clear words about securing the best kind of happiness and treasures in life. Someone strapping a load onto a pickup truck might say, "Don't use all the rope on that old barbecue grill, let's make sure this antique armoire is secure and won't get bumped around!" Jesus gives similar warnings about food, clothing, and hoarding money for ourselves. He once told a story about a rich man who invested lots in his crops and barns but was "not rich in the things of God." His was a sad ending, and Jesus called him a fool.

I hope I can discern between what's temporal and what's eternal so that I don't lose hold of what I want to have with me at the end of my journey.

A thought for today: Are the most important things in life being well guarded in yours?

Fifth Sunday in Lent

Read Mark 1

In the morning, while it was still very dark, he got up and went out to a deserted place, and there he prayed. And Simon and his companions hunted for him. When they found him, they said to him, "Everyone is searching for you." He answered, "Let us go on to the neighboring towns, so that I may proclaim the message there also; for that is what I came out to do." And he went throughout Galilee, proclaiming the message in their synagogues and casting out demons

(Mark 1:35–39)

I didn't want to run last Friday—not so much because of physical fatigue but because of the many other concerns swirling around in my head. It was as if I was walking around in a fog. I began to rationalize.

What's one day? Maybe I'll just go into work. I could get a lot accomplished before the rest of the staff gets there. Perhaps I should just go back to bed for an hour and work out later this afternoon.

That last one, I already knew, rarely works. A person could draw a pretty reliable chart about the likelihood of my working out, by hour of the day. It's not a pretty picture. There would be a steady slope downward until about nine o'clock in the morning, and then a sudden drop-off to 0 percent. If I haven't done it by nine, chances are it's not going to happen.

It was one of those days that I just felt kind of "blah." I hadn't planned my day yet; I was vaguely aware of many things to be done, but I hadn't even listed them all. That was likely a means of avoiding them for at least a while. I eventually realized that the best thing I could do at that moment was to just sit, think, and pray. When I did, I found the words to explain to God—and to myself—what was going on. Eventually, I found the resolve to go out for a run and to pick up a little trash on the way home. It wasn't exhilarating, but I did feel better afterward about following through on my commitment.

The first chapter of Mark's gospel feels like hopping on a fast-moving train from a dead start. John preaches, and then Jesus is baptized, immediately heads off to his temptation in the wilderness, begins preaching, recruits disciples, goes to the synagogue, casts out demons, heals all kinds of folks, goes throughout Galilee preaching and teaching, heals a leper, and deals with crowds that were following him…whew! Perhaps it is no wonder that in the midst of all these, early in the morning Jesus went off on his own to pray.

When Simon and the others found him, they said, "Everyone's looking for you." I'm sure he knew that would be the case. I'm also sure he knew what needed to be taken care of first in order to do what God had called him to do. I hope I can remember that taking time out to pray is often the means to finding the resources needed for the tasks I face.

A thought for today: Before we begin doing, we do well to begin by praying.

Day Twenty-Nine

Monday

Read 2 Peter 1:5–15

For this very reason, you must make every effort to support your faith with goodness, and goodness with knowledge, and knowledge with self-control, and self-control with endurance, and endurance with godliness, and godliness with mutual affection, and mutual affection with love. For if these things are yours and are increasing among you, they keep you from being ineffective and unfruitful in the knowledge of our Lord Jesus Christ.

(2 Peter 1:5–8)

I was on a long stretch of nice, smooth pavement, there was no automobile traffic, and best of all I was really pushing hard on this bike ride. I was near twenty-five miles an hour (fast for cycling), and the stretch ahead made it appear I could keep this up for maybe half a mile.

Wait…what was that?

The one thing a cyclist doesn't want to do at a moment like this is slow down. But I could've sworn I just rode past a wristwatch with the wristband secured to itself the way they are in the display boxes when new.

Doggone it! I had to go back.

Sure enough, it was a wristwatch...but not just any wristwatch. It was the display unit of a heart monitor. I'd never had enough money to purchase one of these. They cost a couple hundred bucks. I picked it up. When I got home, I put a notice on Facebook and on the local bicycle club's website, letting folks know I had found it. I knew than whoever had lost it would surely want it back.

But two weeks passed, and no one responded. So I began to investigate. To make it function as a heart rate monitor, I'd need the chest band. But purchasing one separately was more expensive than getting it in the original box with the wrist display. My son showed some interest in it for a while (he rides too), but he also gave up when he found out how much it would cost to make it fully functional. Without the other part, it was just a wristwatch—the kind you can buy for less than ten dollars.

The scriptures encourage us to grow in our relationship with Christ. A person may have faith, but without growth and exercise, that faith can wither. A person may have a great deal of intelligence and knowledge, but without compassion and discipline those gifts are of little use.

The second epistle of Peter encourages us to "keep on adding" so that our knowledge of Christ doesn't become ineffective. Heart needs hands. Rationality needs spirit. Individual needs community, and vice versa. May God help us keep on growing so that we have what we need to function as Christ's disciples.

A thought for today: Am I growing in the ways that can make me more functional for Christ's sake?

Tuesday

Read Matthew 6: 24–33

No one can serve two masters; for a slave will either hate the one and love the other, or be devoted to the one and despise the other. You cannot serve God and wealth.

(Matthew 6:24)

"Cha-ching!" Today I hit the trash-picker-upper jackpot: a bag that could be used to put trash in the rest of the way home. It was one of those thin, plastic bags from Wal-Mart that just sort of came floating down the street, straight toward me. All I had to do was bend over and pick it up, and I was set.

I picked up two smashed beer cans from the street and tossed them in. Then a Styrofoam cup, lid, and straw from Sonic. A cigarette package. An advertising circular. A soft drink can (I smashed it myself before dropping it in). The bag was beginning to fill up.

I continued on. Some more stuff stuffed in. And some more...and some more. I didn't want to miss a single thing. And then, the inevitable happened: the bag split from too much weight or stretching and all the contents fell out at my feet. What had begun as a great opportunity ended up as a mess of my own creation.

But I've known what that's like in other areas of my life as well. Spreading ourselves too thin, we call it. Whether it's time or money or energy, we spend these resources on too many things. There's a clearly mandated focus at work, and I allow other, less important tasks to commandeer my time. We even do it to our relationships, not realizing that the distractions that take us away from our spouse or our children are leading toward a split of another kind...in some cases, leaving a painful mess at our feet. What sometimes begin as great opportunities or pleasant pastimes can become harsh masters demanding our resources, attention, and devotion.

Jesus encouraged us to pay special attention to the things that matter most and to not be deceived by the seeming importance of things that in the long range do not bring true happiness. Maybe I can recall the lesson of the bag I split and remain happy to carry around inside me what's most important of all.

A thought for today: The most important things in life are often those that cry out least for our attention when neglected.

Day Thirty-One

Wednesday

Read Genesis 1:28–31

God blessed them, and God said to them, "Be fruit-
ful and multiply, and fill the earth and subdue it; and
have dominion over the fish of the sea and over the
birds of the air and over every living thing that moves
upon the earth."

(Genesis 1:28)

I am fascinated by the variety of arguments and conclusions drawn by individuals as they seek to understand the Bible's story of creation and the fall. Sincere, well-meaning people on different sides see things so differently! Some believe the six-day creation story is to be taken as fact, a narrative as journalistically accurate as the newspaper story that tells who, what, when, how, where, and why. Others view the narrative as a metaphor or myth, an etiological story that tries to put words to something that is and will forever remain beyond our understanding.

The same is true for the next story in the Bible, of the fall of human-kind. Some see the serpent in the garden as the personification of Satan, and thus sin entered a previously sinless world. Others view it as true and sacred scripture, but probably not factually true. There are two points, however, that I believe would be affirmed by those at either pole of these sometimes contentious differences (and by the many more in between): that God is the creator of a good world and that human beings have taken the earth for granted and messed it up.

Stewardship of the earth is not something peripheral to Christian theology. In fact, the first thing we are told about the relationship between God and humans is that we are given responsibility and power to subdue the earth. The second creation story (Genesis 2, in which Eve was made out of Adam's rib) tells us that the man was put in the Garden of Eden to tend it and watch over it (Genesis 2:15). Again, at this point, both liberals and conservatives agree that the Garden is emblematic of the earth itself...a place we are given to live and which we are to tend and watch.

Picking up trash at the end of my run does not solve the problem of global warming, nor does it reduce the threat of nuclear disasters such as Chernobyl or Fukushima. It does remind me, however, that this is where I live, and I bear some responsibility for it. This is not only because of how I interpret the Bible's story of creation but also because of logic. Where else is there? Marshall McLuhan's prediction of a "global village" has come to pass, and what used to seem a world away is not.

> **A thought for today: We do not inherit the earth from our ancestors; we borrow it from our children.**

Day Thirty-Two

Thursday

Read John 8:1–11

"Teacher," they said to Jesus, "this woman was caught in the act of adultery. The law of Moses says to stone her. What do you say?"

(John 8:4–5 NLT)

By now, anyone who has read more than a few of these devotionals will know that sometimes I take the trash to the Dumpster, but sometimes I bring it into the house or garage because to me it's not trash.

The bungee cords, the art canvas waiting to be repainted, the occasional thingamajig I decide has not outlived its purpose…it's not that I'm a hoarder. It's more than likely due to my own history of not being tossed out.

I've had addiction problems, money problems, and relationship problems, and I've made so many mistakes along the way. There have been so many times I could have been dismissed, caught, written up, or beaten down. But I've been fortunate. I've encountered people of grace who hoped I could be better than I was in whatever moment those bad things were happening.

Jesus was like that. Seems to me his standard for beginning as a follower of his was remarkably low, even though the standard to which he said we should aspire was to "become perfect, even as your Father in heaven is perfect." Tax collector? Fine. Samaritan? Fine. Woman? Fine. Divorced? Okay. Roman officer? Sure, I can work with that. Blind? No problem. Leprosy? Let's see what we can do about that. Adulteress? Well, that's your past. Let's talk about your future.

They were ready to throw away the life of the woman who made a mistake and got caught. Jesus shows us the difference—and it's a big, amazing, wonderful difference—between how people often react to such errors and how God views them.

Yes, I see trash differently than other people do. May God help me continue to do so.

> ***A thought for today: We all have a past. With Jesus, we also have a future.***

Friday

Read Luke 19:1–10

Zacchaeus stood there and said to the Lord, "Look,
half of my possessions, Lord, I will give to the poor;
and if I have defrauded anyone of anything, I will pay
back four times as much." Then Jesus said to him,
"Today salvation has come to this house, because he
too is a son of Abraham. For the Son of Man came to
seek out and to save the lost."

(Luke 19:8–10)

My experience in recovery and as a part of various twelve-step groups has allowed me to see and read the scriptures in a new way. Take, for example, the story of Zacchaeus.

I think perhaps Zacchaeus had hit his bottom. Whatever his particular addiction was (the story makes it seem that perhaps money was part of it, but sometimes people focus on money so they can satisfy other itches), the story indicates he was ready for a change. One of the biggest hurdles that alcoholics and other addicts must overcome is their fear of being seen or that others may find out they are going to a twelve-step meeting. Zacchaeus climbs a tree. Ostensibly this is to see Jesus (the text indicates that one or the other of them was short), but perhaps it was so Jesus would see him. His need was greater than his embarrassment.

He's ready. He's ready to make amends and change his ways, which is what the twelve-step process is about. It's downright amazing that in his short statement Zacchaeus admits his need, confesses (in general) his wrong, and becomes willing to make amends—all of which are part of the twelve-step program.

Whether it's making a change in our stewardship of the planet, beginning to pick up the pieces of relationships we've messed up, or being "four times" more committed to whatever path of salvation the Lord has put in front of us (and from which we may have strayed), it's a celebrative occasion when we experience a day of turnaround the way Zacchaeus did. When it happens to us, I think Jesus might once again say, "Today salvation has come to this house...for the Son of Man came to seek out and to save the lost."

> **A thought for today: What might happen if we made amends and changed our ways? Are we ready to?**

Day Thirty-Four

Saturday

Read Mark 11:1–11

Many people spread their cloaks on the road, and others spread leafy branches that they had cut in the fields. Then those who went ahead and those who followed were shouting,
"Hosanna!
Blessed is the one who comes in the name of the Lord!
Blessed is the coming kingdom of our ancestor David!
Hosanna in the highest heaven!"

(Mark 11:8–10)

Very early one morning I was feeling particularly energetic. I mowed and edged the lawn, I ranged out beyond the curb and picked up little bits of glass and a couple of smashed cans that had found their way to the lowest part of the pavement on both my side of the street and that of my across-the-street neighbor. I noticed there was some gravel that had also found its way to the curb. I decided to sweep and scoop up what I could.

I wasn't too far into the job when I realized it was a *draa-a-a-g*! The little bits of gravel and asphalt weren't easy to sweep into piles, even with my stiff-bristled push broom. And then, scooping up the piles of gravel with the snow shovel (its flat edge worked better than my digging shovel), it seemed each scoop must have weighed five pounds or more. I'd transferred maybe ten scoops into the trash bin when I heard a low hum in the distance. I looked down the street and saw the city's big street sweeper slowly, methodically making its way toward me.

I collected my tools, tossed them on the lawn, and pulled the trash bin out of the road as I slowly waited, watched, and then marveled at my good fortune. That street sweeper did a much better job at sweeping up the dust, rocks, and grit than I did. I just needed to get out of his way and let him do what he was sent to do.

Tomorrow begins Holy Week. It's a special time when we recall Jesus entering Jerusalem for what would be the final week before his crucifixion. As he entered the city that day, to the welcoming sounds of the crowd, I wonder if they could have possibly known that he was about to do what no prophet or priest ever could. Whenever we're tempted to try to earn our salvation, I hope we'll recall that God sent someone to take care of all that. We just need to let him do what he was sent to do.

A thought for today: So much in our lives can weigh us down in ways we can't fix. Let's be glad that Jesus shows us a way to let those things go.

Palm/Passion Sunday

Read Matthew 21

Jesus said to them, "Have you never read in the scriptures:
'The stone that the builders rejected
has become the cornerstone;
this was the Lord's doing,
and it is amazing in our eyes'?
Therefore I tell you, the kingdom of God will be taken
away from you and given to a people that produces
the fruits of the kingdom. The one who falls on this
stone will be broken to pieces; and it will crush any-
one on whom it falls."
When the chief priests and the Pharisees heard his
parables, they realized that he was speaking about
them. They wanted to arrest him, but they feared the
crowds, because they regarded him as a prophet.

(Matthew 21:42–46)

I have a friend who is head of a bicycle advocacy program in one of America's largest cities. In her own way, she's trying to clean up the world and make people's lives better. The breadth of her work is amazing. Her organization works for increased access to bicycles, dedicated bicycle infrastructure (lanes, trails, parking, etc.), and political advocacy. One-third of the people in her city lack access to a car, so her work helps with social and economic mobility as well. It's amazing work.

But wow, does she have to fight! It's not that people are against her; it's just that she's trying to change minds and situations that have been formed around cars and automobile-based lifestyles. People want change, but they often don't want *to* change.

When I read the story of Jesus's entry into Jerusalem on Palm Sunday, I have no doubt he knew that he would meet with resistance. The people wanted change, I'm sure. That's why he was welcomed by many. But Jerusalem was the political and religious center of the country. And those who work to change the powers that be often discover it's a difficult path.

Maybe I need to step up my game a bit. I'm not eager to meet resistance, but maybe it's time to invite others to join in the trash pickup habit. Maybe I need to see if others in my neighborhood might help. I imagine some people won't be too crazy about the idea. But it's those who forge ahead, despite the odds, who so often make a difference in the world. Some will join, some will not. But just like God's work of redemption, what is accomplished in the end is worth the fight.

A thought for today: What do you care about enough to fight for, even if it's a long, uphill struggle?

Day Thirty-Five

Monday of Holy Week

Read Mark 11:15–19

Then they came to Jerusalem. And he entered the temple and began to drive out those who were selling and those who were buying in the temple, and he overturned the tables of the money changers and the seats of those who sold doves; and he would not allow anyone to carry anything through the temple. He was teaching and saying, "Is it not written, 'My house shall be called a house of prayer for all the nations'? But you have made it a den of robbers."

(Mark 11:15–17)

The account of Jesus overturning the tables of the moneychangers in the Temple creates something of a theological dilemma for Christians. We're faced with the idea that either Jesus blew his cool and lost his temper or that his actions show how stirring things up in a "zero tolerance" kind of way is sometimes appropriate. The church throughout the ages has opted for the second of these possibilities.

When friends and families join in an intervention to save an addict (and to make hard, bottom line decisions about consequences if the addict doesn't get help); when oppressed people strike, march, or join in nonviolent protest; when pastors call attention to societal sin and the need for justice; or even in politics when people overthrow an unjust government (and let's not forget that the United States was founded through a revolution) there are times when a hard line must be drawn. To be tolerant any longer would imply complicity. Tables must be tossed.

The image of our planet's pollution has been used throughout these Lenten devotionals. Scientists tell us that some firm decisions and changes must be made soon if we are to prevent disaster. But the same is also true for other aspects of our lives—it's just that we don't usually have someone analyzing things and warning us about where we're heading. In fact, the pollution of our planet is simply another manifestation of our real problem—our inability (or refusal) to hear and follow God's word.

There's a time when God's people getting riled up is the way God works. If Jesus were here talking to me about my life, would he find reason to raise his voice or pound his fist on the table? If we invited him to lead your church, would he "overturn a few tables" in budgeting, teaching, or programming?

A thought for today: Are you nearing a slippery slope in some area of your life that you need to address in a decisive way, and right now?

Tuesday of Holy Week

Read Mark 14:1–9

But Jesus said, "Let her alone; why do you trouble her? She has performed a good service for me. For you always have the poor with you, and you can show kindness to them whenever you wish; but you will not always have me. She has done what she could; she has anointed my body beforehand for its burial. Truly I tell you, wherever the good news is proclaimed in the whole world, what she has done will be told in remembrance of her."

(Mark 14:6–9)

We are just a few days from the end of Lent. For some, it has been a time of salvation, repentance, and renewed faithfulness. For many others—in fact, most people in the world—the season has come and gone with little or no notice.

I have picked up a few pieces of trash during Lent and have told others about a few of the ways my trash habit has led to spiritual discoveries and insights. And still, there is trash. There is deadly conflict between the children of Abraham called Jew, Christian, and Muslim. There is greed and war. There is sex trafficking of children. One of these days I will die (as will you) and these things will likely still persist. Why try?

We try because Jesus takes notice of our acts of love, compassion, and concern. When a woman (variously identified in different gospels and traditions) extravagantly anointed Jesus's feet, it did not prevent his tragic death. But he noticed, and he pointed to the power of her loving action: "wherever the good news is proclaimed in the whole world, what she has done will be told in remembrance of her."

And so we, like her and like Jesus, place our efforts into God's hands. Somehow we believe that our efforts are not wasted and do not go unnoticed by the One who matters most.

A thought for today: When we have the opportunity, let's follow this woman's example and love extravagantly, believing it will be remembered.

Day Thirty-Seven

Wednesday of Holy Week

Read John 13:21–30

After saying this Jesus was troubled in spirit, and declared, "Very truly, I tell you, one of you will betray me." The disciples looked at one another, uncertain of whom he was speaking.

(John 13:21–22)

A friend of mine gave me permission to share a story he related to me several years ago.

He and some of his fraternity brothers from college days had arranged a reunion trip to Las Vegas to reminisce, play golf, and party together. Things started off well enough until the second day. The organizer of the trip had arranged for some fun that involved drugs and some prostitutes. My friend realized that while there had been a time in his life when he may have gone along with the schedule, that behavior was especially inappropriate for men who were husbands and dads, as he and several of the others were. He told me, "I sat there in my hotel thinking about how angry I was that he had sprung this on me, and then I stood up and said out loud, "Dammit, I'm a Christian!" (a sentence that I'm guessing is rarely spoken anywhere). He packed his bag, checked out of the hotel, and flew home.

My own theology doesn't allow me to believe Judas was born for the role he played in Jesus's crucifixion. I have to believe that he somehow became willing, for whatever reasons, to betray his friend. And isn't that the way it is with so much of the trash in our lives and our souls? We would like to blame someone else, but even those who have truly been victimized are given the opportunity to forgive, recover, and lean on God's Spirit for the power and direction we so often need.

We, like the blind man Jesus healed of his infirmity, need to be healed of our inability to see our complacency and complicity. We need to be helped to see the power God offers to (in the words of my church's baptismal vows) "resist evil, injustice and oppression in whatever forms they may present themselves." Even when the hour seems late and the evil powers of this world are in full motion, we can choose to not give in to giving up. I think it would be wonderful if there were more people declaring, "Dammit, I'm a Christian" and saying no to going along.

> *A thought for today: God has promised to help us in times of temptation and trial. Pause. Pray. And let God lead you.*

Thursday of Holy Week

Mark 14:26–50

And going a little farther, he threw himself on the ground and prayed that, if it were possible, the hour might pass from him. He said, "Abba, Father, for you all things are possible; remove this cup from me; yet, not what I want, but what you want."

(Mark 14:35–36)

There are some theologians who have identified the high point in the drama of Jesus's death not at Golgotha but at the Garden of Gethsemane. After reading their work, I understand their point.

These Christian thinkers are not discounting the awful events of Jesus's trial, scourging, and crucifixion. They still hold the cross as the central symbol of our Lord and faith. Rather, they are pointing to the way that Jesus's faithfulness to God was most sorely tried as he prayed in the garden. It was in that moment of trusting God completely—with his life and anything that came along with doing God's will—that those other events became predictable outcomes. Jesus's fate on the cross was sealed by his faithfulness in the garden.

It is not likely that any of us will ever face such a time of testing. But in the moment we give ourselves into God's hands as completely as we can, other events will follow. They may be costly to us in terms of our time, money, or energy. Whether it's picking up trash, visiting someone who is homebound, volunteering in a local school or hospital, or visiting prisoners in jail, once we decide to do God's will no matter what the cost, the die is cast. The good news is that we will find power and the spiritual strength to endure hardship, loneliness, and even betrayal.

A thought for today: The core of Christian discipleship is "not my will, but thine."

Day Thirty-Nine

Friday of Holy Week (Good Friday)

Read John 19:16–42

So they took Jesus; and carrying the cross by himself, he went out to what is called The Place of the Skull, which in Hebrew is called Golgotha. There they crucified him, and with him two others, one on either side, with Jesus between them. Pilate also had an inscription written and put on the cross. It read, "Jesus of Nazareth, the King of the Jews."

(John 19:16–19)

I cannot unsee the trash I used to not see. The habit of looking and noticing it has, in some ways, made my life a bit more inconvenient, but it has added purpose and meaning to those moments when I see and sense myself called to decide what to do. Seeing and noticing has given me the opportunity to be part of the solution, not just an oblivious part of the problem.

Likewise is the image of Jesus on the cross. Seeing this sight—whether with our eyes or in our imaginations, through art or music, in our hearts or souls—makes our lives a bit more inconvenient, but it also adds meaning, purpose, and understanding. Somehow this salvific moment of divine encounter between the Son of God and the forces of evil sums up our situation. It also calls us to see, decide, and respond as nothing else can. If we've truly "seen" Jesus on the cross, I'm not sure we can ever unsee it.

The cross is inexhaustible in its meaning and forever contemporary in its relevance. In the narrative of Jesus's crucifixion, we see humanity—our weakness, scheming, and short-sightedness; our betrayals and denials; our changeability and our repeatedly putting to death the goodness and truth of God. We also see the love of God, the pain and suffering of God, and the pitiful saga of human ignorance and hubris taken up into the merciful power of God.

Today is Good Friday. It is solemn and straightforward in its presentation of the situation. It is also hopeful in its claims that not even death will defeat God's purposes. The God who created this earth and who has suffered in all times and places with its peoples is the God who will also not abandon us to ourselves. We dare not unsee the cross and its pain, because in it we see the inexhaustible love of God.

A thought for today: The cross of Christ will never cease to speak to us, call to us, and guide us.

Day Forty

(Easter Vigil)

Read John 19:31–42

After these things, Joseph of Arimathea, who was a disciple of Jesus, though a secret one because of his fear of the Jews, asked Pilate to let him take away the body of Jesus. Pilate gave him permission; so he came and removed his body. Nicodemus, who had at first come to Jesus by night, also came, bringing a mixture of myrrh and aloes, weighing about a hundred pounds.

(John 19:38–39)

There is hardly a more courageous act in the entire Bible than the one lovingly performed by Joseph of Arimathea and Nicodemus. We must remember than when they came forward to claim the body of Jesus, they were identifying with a rejected, peasant criminal who was considered an enemy of both the state and their faith. Their lives would no doubt be different in some unpleasant ways from this moment on. And yet they came forward.

They knew nothing of the resurrection; they received no accolades for the way they provided for Jesus. But they showed themselves to be men of conviction and fortitude. At this moment, Jesus was not a winner; he was a loser. But he had touched them, and they would not allow that to be forgotten. Criminals' bodies were often either left to rot on crosses (as a deterrent to crime) or thrown on the city's ever-smoldering trash heap. These men would not allow the body of Jesus to be treated as trash.

Today, we wait. We wait for tomorrow, when we celebrate the resurrection of our Lord, but we also wait for the coming of his Kingdom. It has begun in our midst and in this world, but it awaits its culmination in the victory of our God, a victory that is already won. As we wait, let us work, and trust, and love—as our Lord has taught us. And let's be courageous as we do so, claiming him in all we say and do.

A thought for today: Christ has died; Christ is risen; Christ will come again.

Notes and Reflections

Notes and Reflections

Notes and Reflections

Notes and Reflections

Notes and Reflections

Notes and Reflections

Notes and Reflections

Notes and Reflections

Notes and Reflections

Notes and Reflections

Notes and Reflections

Notes and Reflections

Made in the USA
Columbia, SC
02 February 2019